# Best of
# Ronan Tynan

Piano/Vocal arrangements by William Lewis

Photography by Merri Cyr

Cherry Lane Music Company
Director of Publications/Project Supervisor: Mark Phillips

ISBN 1-57560-826-X

Visit our website at www.cherrylane.com

# Ronan Tynan

*"Put courage in your dreams, Ronan, and leave the rest to the Man Above, and then you will carve your footprints in the sand."*

These words have shaped the remarkable life of the Irish tenor Ronan Tynan—a proud and loving lesson of his mother's—from his childhood milking cows on a farm in County Kilkenny, Ireland, to an ever-evolving career as a singer, bringing him worldwide fame and admiration that could have existed only in the farthest reaches of those dreams. International audiences met Tynan as a member of the Irish Tenors. Now his singular voice and irresistible appeal have led him to strike out on his own, a decision that seems to have resulted in something far more meaningful than a mere solo career.

Perhaps you already know Ronan Tynan's voice.

U2's Bono knows it. "When Ronan sings the clouds cry but the sun turns up sooner than it would have," he has written, in a liner note for *Ronan*, the tenor's new recording for Decca. "He sang for my father, Bob, as we put him in the ground, and it felt like shelter. The wind died down, the rain stopped for the loudest, softest voice we have…a great Irish tenor."

Tynan's singing offered the gentlest consolation at the funeral of President Ronald Reagan in the summer of 2004, when an international TV audience of more than 35 million heard him sing "Amazing Grace" and

Schubert's "Ave Maria" at the personal invitation of Nancy Reagan.

If you're a fan of the New York Yankees—and Tynan himself is, big time—you might have heard him peal out one of his unforgettable performances of "God Bless America" in the seventh inning stretch of a big game, as he frequently does.

In the wake of 9/11, the men and women of the New York Police Department and New York Fire Department and their families have been able to count on Ronan Tynan's abiding concern and beautiful voice. He has performed at benefits and memorial services for New York's Finest and Bravest, and his singing has softened the sorrow at many a funeral in the wake of the tragedy.

There are plenty of joyous moments, as well. In the spring of 2004, the Belmont Stakes got off to a rollicking start when Tynan—himself a passionate horseman—christened the race with a ringing rendition of "New York, New York." He sang at the wedding of New York's former mayor Rudolph Giuliani to Judith Nathan on the grounds of Gracie Mansion. His voice brightened the 80th birthday celebration of former President George H.W. Bush last summer in Houston. He gives motivational speeches all over the country. He has played Feinstein's, one of the New York's poshest cabaret rooms. And the spring 2005 release of his new self-titled CD, the first in a new exclusive agreement with Universal Music's Decca label, begins a new chapter in his amazing story.

"I think it shows a greater versatility than any other album I've done," Tynan says of the recording. "For the first time I'm singing material that has tremendous depth and weight. I wanted to sing a greater variety of music and spread my wings a bit, make a move out of the classic 'Irish tenor' vein."

Ronan Tynan is barely out of his thirties, yet he has already overcome formidable personal challenges and achieved the kind of success only a mother could have wished for him. Though he had always sung as a boy, he did not seriously consider formal voice study until he was 33, when he was well into his residency as a physician. The success he quickly found as a singer is a typical development in a life of extraordinary achievement. Born with lower limb disability that might have sidelined him, Tynan was still "as wild as a March hare" when he was a growing boy, riding horses and racing motorcycles. When he was 20, his legs had to be amputated below the knee after an auto accident caused serious complications. Just weeks after the operation, he was climbing up the steps of his college dorm. Within a year, he was winning gold medals in the Paralympics as a multitalented athlete. Between 1981 and 1984, Tynan amassed 18 gold medals and 14 world records.

Such determination—reinforced by his steadfast parents, a diminutive couple with gigantic ambitions for their son—soon propelled him to conquer a whole new field. Tynan became the first disabled person ever admitted to the National College of Physical Education, and then a full-fledged medical doctor, specializing in orthopedic sports injuries, with a degree from prestigious Trinity College. He won both the John McCormack Cup for Tenor Voice and the BBC talent show *Go for It* less than one year after beginning the study of voice. The following year, he won the International Operatic Singing Competition in Maumarde, France. He made his operatic debut as Pinkerton in Puccini's *Madama Butterfly* and cut his teeth on the concert repertoire in performances of Verdi's *Requiem*, Mendelssohn's *Elijah*, Handel's *Messiah*, Rossini's *Stabat Mater*, and Puccini's *Messa di Gloria*. In 1998 Tynan joined Anthony Kearns and John McDermott (later Finbar Wright) as the Irish Tenors, an instant worldwide sensation. His autobiography, *Halfway Home*, was published in February of 2001.

Collaborating on *Ronan* with producer Nick Patrick—the man behind the great recordings of Russell Watson, Amici Forever, and Dominic Miller—Tynan sings powerful hymns of the spirit such as "Amazing Grace" and "How Great Thou Art." With the assistance of his friend Margaret Byrne, he has written the heartfelt "Passing Through" to honor his mother, whose vibrant spirit has been taken away by the long night of Alzheimer's disease. The recording also includes the bristling title song from the musical *Man of La Mancha*, the pop classic "From a Distance," a prayerful aria from a beloved Spanish zarzuela ("La roca fría del Calvario" from Serrano's *La Dolorosa*), a great film theme that has become a song—"Mansions of the Lord" (from *We Were Soldiers*)—as well as several new songs created especially for the recording. Some of the assorted and well-known writers of the original tracks include Richard Marx, Desmond Child, Aldo Nova, Gary Burr, and Jeff Cohen.

"I want to reach everyone with this album," Tynan says.

The big Irishman has a special relationship with American audiences now, and he considers New York "my home away from home."

"New York is powerful and intense, and it begs you to take it on," Tynan marvels. "If you do that and do it right, it will give you absolutely everything you want. The thing I love about New York and the States is that there are so many people who want you to do well. They *will* you to do well. They encourage you and they rejoice in your success. That's a great virtue. I think Americans are fantastic people, amazing. I think they can stand up and be proud and hold their heads high, and if others don't get it…well, it's *their* problem. I am so grateful. And I'll never forget that America has given me so much more than I'll ever be able to give back."

# CONTENTS

The reason I selected these songs is simply that they bring great happiness to me whenever I performed them. Each time I sing them, they bring back different memories to me, and many of these memories are associated with concert performances all over the USA.

I have been blessed with a gift from God, and each of the writers of these songs has been given an amazing talent. This gift and these talents must be shared with all of you.

Accompanist Bill Lewis has done an amazing job with these arrangements, and those of you who know Bill know he's one of nature's finest gentlemen. God bless you all and enjoy playing these great songs.

# Amazing Grace

Words by
John Newton

Traditional American Melody

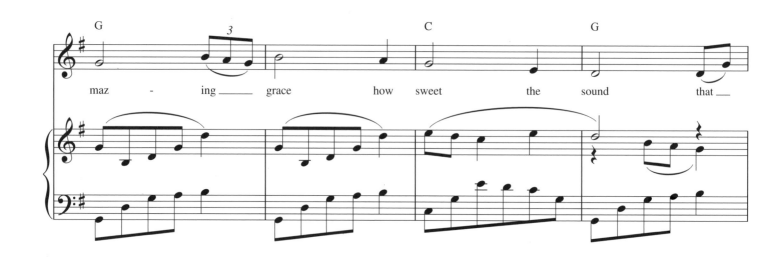

maz - ing ___ grace how sweet the sound that ___

saved a ___ wretch like ___ me. I ___

sing God's praise than __ when we __ first be - gun. _____ A -

maz - ing __ grace how sweet the sound that __ saved a __

wretch like __ me. _____ I __ once was __ lost but

now am found. Was __ blind but __ now I see. _____

*rall.*

9

# Ave Maria

By Franz Schubert

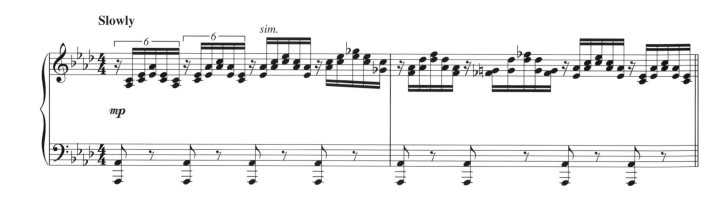

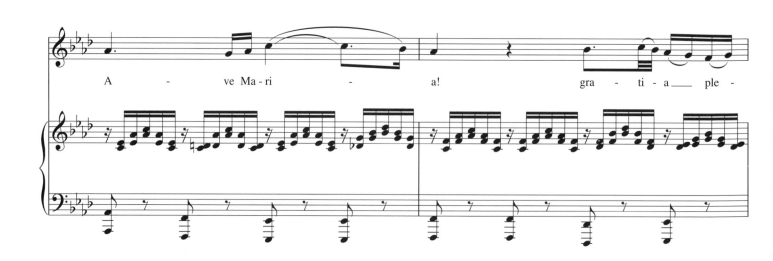

na. A - ve! A - ve! Do - mi - nus, Do - mi - nus te-cum. Be-ne-

dic - ta tu in mu - li-e - ri-bus et be - ne - dic - tus, et

be - ne-dic - tus fruc-tus ven - tris, ven-tris tu - i Je - sus.

A - ve Ma - ri - a!

ho - ra mor - tis no - strae, in ho - ra mor - tis, mor - tis no - strae, in

ho - ra mor - tis no - strae. A - ve Ma - ri -

a!

dim.

p

# Danny Boy

Words by
Frederick Edward Weatherly

Traditional Irish Folk Melody

back    when sum-mer's in the    mead - ow, _____ or when the val - ley's hushed and white with

snow.       'Tis I'll be there       in sun - shine or in       shad - ow. _____ Oh Dan - ny

Boy, oh Dan - ny Boy, I love you    so.

And when you    come    and all the flow'rs are    dy - ing, ____ if I am dead,    as dead I well may

# From a Distance

Words and Music by
Julie Gold

Coda

heart _____ of ev - 'ry _____ man. _____ It's the hope of __ hopes, _ it's the love of __ loves. _ This is the song of __ ev - 'ry _ man. God _ is watch-ing us. __ God _ is watch-ing us. __ God _ is watch-ing us from a __ dis - tance. _____ God _ is

1.

2.

watch-ing us from a dis - tance. _____

# God Bless America

Words and Music by
Irving Berlin

Stand be-side her ____ and guide her ____

through the night with a light from a-bove. ____

From the moun - tains ____ to the prai - ries, ____

to the o - ceans ____ white with foam, ____

23

# Grace

Words and Music by
Frank O'Meara and Sean O'Meara

in your arms ___ and let this mo - ment lin - ger. ___

They take me out at dawn and I will die. ___

___ With - out my love I place this wed - ding

ring up - on your fin - ger. ___ There won't be time to

# I'll Take You Home Again, Kathleen

Words and Music by
Thomas Westendorf

Moderately, with expression

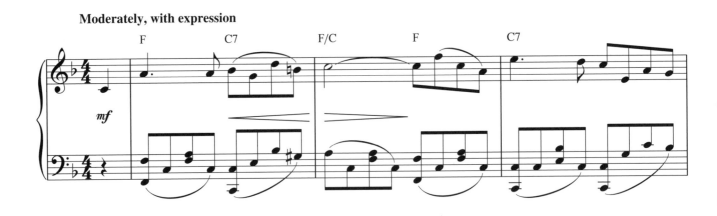

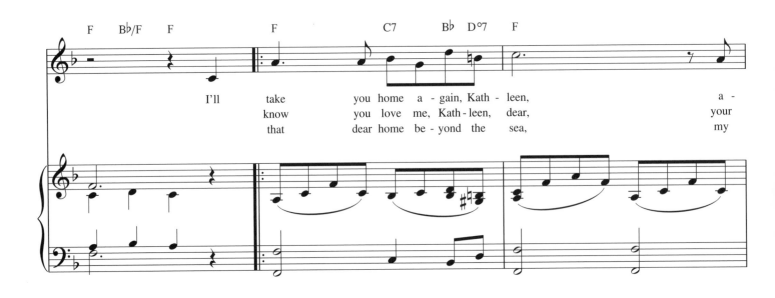

I'll take you home a-gain, Kath-leen,
know you love me, Kath-leen, dear,
that dear home be-yond the sea,

a -
your
my

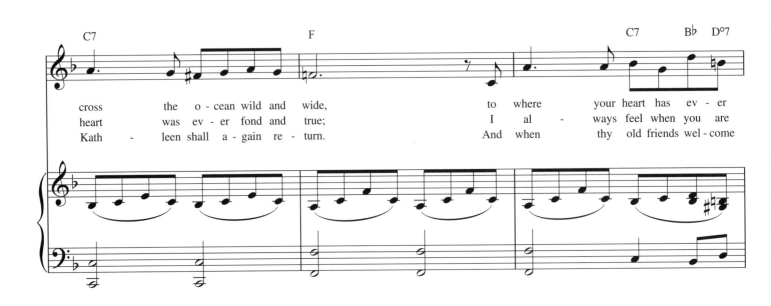

cross the o - cean wild and wide,
heart was ev - er fond and true;
Kath - leen shall a - gain re - turn.

to where your heart has ev - er
I al - ways feel when you are
And when thy old friends wel - come

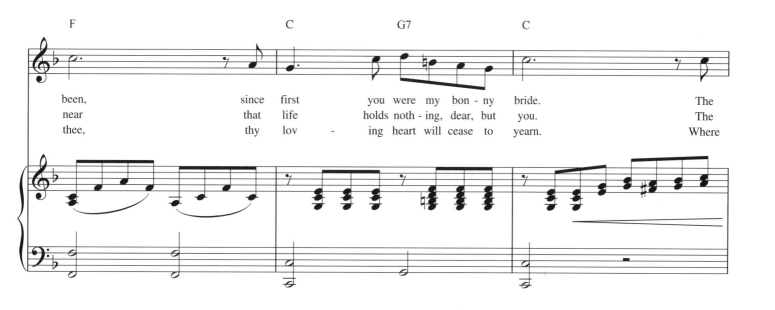

been,     since first     you were my bon - ny bride.     The
near     that life     holds noth - ing, dear, but you.     The
thee,     thy lov - ing heart will cease to yearn.     Where

ros - es all have left your cheek,     I've watched     them fade a - way and
smiles     that once you gave to me,     I scarce - ly ev - er see them
laughs     the lit - tle sil - ver stream,     be - side     your moth - er's hum - ble

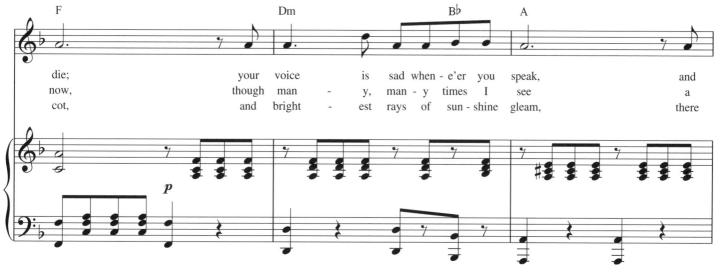

die;     your voice     is sad when - e'er you speak,     and
now,     though man - y, man - y times I see     a
cot,     and bright - est rays of sun - shine gleam,     there

# Isle of Hope, Isle of Tears

Words and Music by
Brendan Graham

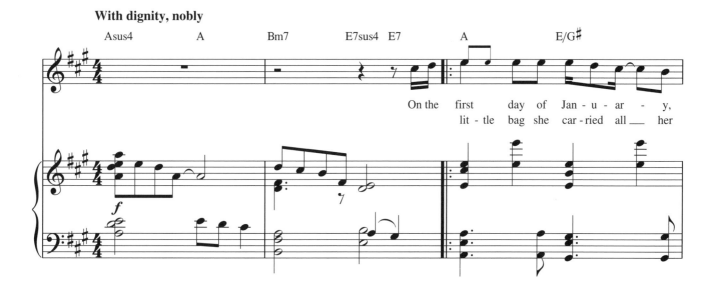

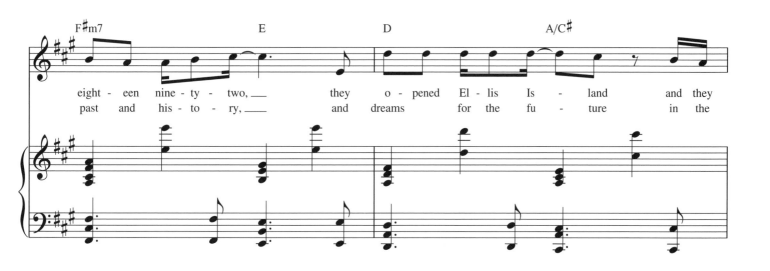

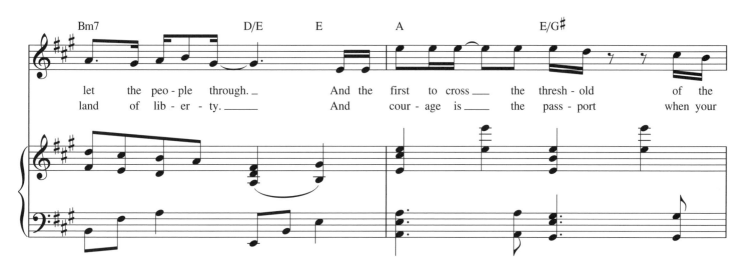

33

Isle of hope _ and tears _ was An - nie Moore _ from Ire - land, _ who was all of fif - teen
old world dis - ap - pears. _ 'Cause there's no fu - ture in the past _ when you're fif - teen

years. ___
years. ___ Isle of hope, isle of tears, isle of free - dom, isle of fears, _ but it's

not the isle _ I left be - hind, ___ that isle of hun - ger, isle of pain, isle you'll

nev - er see a - gain, but the isle of home _ is al - ways on your mind. In her

mind. When they closed down El - lis Is - land in nine - teen for - ty - three, sev - en - teen mil - lion peo - ple had come there for sanc - tuar - y. And it's spring - time when I came here and I stepped on - to its pier. I thought of how it must have been when you're on - ly fif - teen years. Isle of isle of home is al - ways on your mind.

# La roca fría del Calvario

By José Serrano and Juan José Lorente

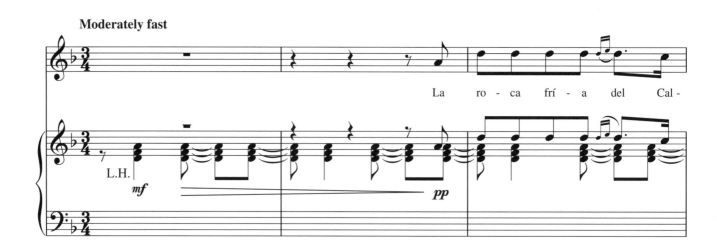

do - bla al pe - so de la pe - na; pe - ro si - gue_a - de -

lan - te. Ca - mi - na, y sus la - bios de hie - lo be - san al

sue - lo, don - de bro - ta_u - na flor en ca - da go - ta de

san - gre de - rra - ma - da por Je - sús el Re - den -

*mf*

*f*

*rall.*

# My Irish Molly-O

Traditional

# My Wild Irish Rose

Words and Music by
Chauncey Olcott

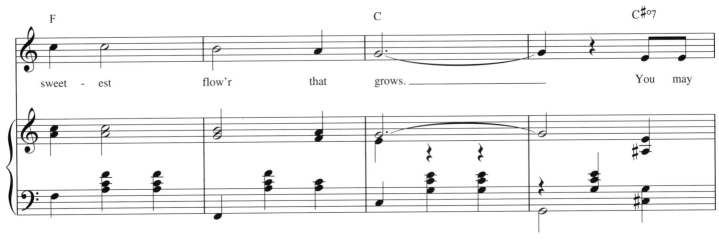

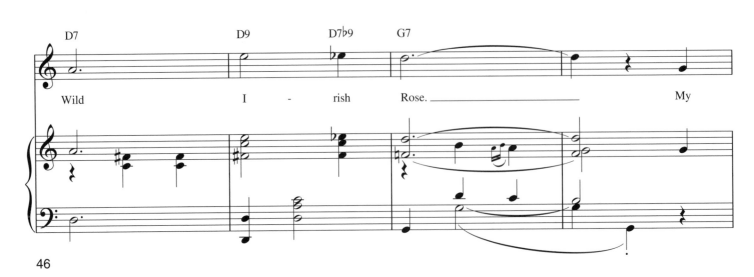

# When You Were Sweet Sixteen

Words and Music by
James Thornton

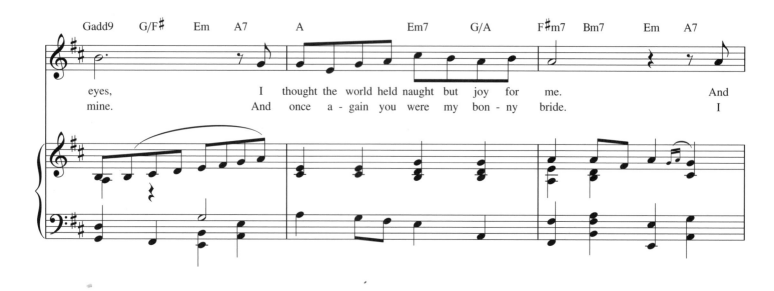

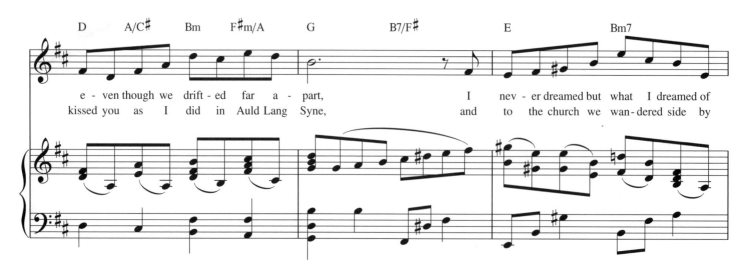

# Will Ye Go, Lassie, Go

Words and Music by
The McPeake Family

# You Raise Me Up

Words and Music by
Brendan Graham and Rolf Lovland

# More Great Piano/Vocal Books

## FROM CHERRY LANE

For a complete listing of Cherry Lane titles available,
including contents listings, please visit our web site at
**www.cherrylane.com**

| | | |
|---|---|---|
| 02500343 | Almost Famous | $14.95 |
| 02502171 | The Best of Boston | $17.95 |
| 02500672 | Black Eyed Peas – Elephunk | $17.95 |
| 02500665 | Sammy Cahn Songbook | $24.95 |
| 02500144 | Mary Chapin Carpenter – Party Doll & Other Favorites | $16.95 |
| 02502163 | Mary Chapin Carpenter – Stones in the Road | $17.95 |
| 02502165 | John Denver Anthology – Revised | $22.95 |
| 02502227 | John Denver – A Celebration of Life | $14.95 |
| 02500002 | John Denver Christmas | $14.95 |
| 02502166 | John Denver's Greatest Hits | $17.95 |
| 02502151 | John Denver – A Legacy in Song (Softcover) | $24.95 |
| 02502152 | John Denver – A Legacy in Song (Hardcover) | $34.95 |
| 02500566 | Poems, Prayers and Promises: The Art and Soul of John Denver | $19.95 |
| 02500326 | John Denver – The Wildlife Concert | $17.95 |
| 02500501 | John Denver and the Muppets: A Christmas Together | $9.95 |
| 02509922 | The Songs of Bob Dylan | $29.95 |
| 02500586 | Linda Eder – Broadway My Way | $14.95 |
| 02500497 | Linda Eder – Gold | $14.95 |
| 02500396 | Linda Eder – Christmas Stays the Same | $17.95 |
| 02500175 | Linda Eder – It's No Secret Anymore | $14.95 |
| 02502209 | Linda Eder – It's Time | $17.95 |
| 02500630 | Donald Fagen – 5 of the Best | $7.95 |
| 02500535 | Erroll Garner Anthology | $19.95 |
| 02500270 | Gilbert & Sullivan for Easy Piano | $12.95 |
| 02500318 | Gladiator | $12.95 |
| 02500273 | Gold & Glory: The Road to El Dorado | $16.95 |
| 02502126 | Best of Guns N' Roses | $17.95 |
| 02502072 | Guns N' Roses – Selections from Use Your Illusion I and II | $17.95 |
| 02500014 | Sir Roland Hanna Collection | $19.95 |
| 02500352 | Hanson – This Time Around | $16.95 |
| 02502134 | Best of Lenny Kravitz | $12.95 |
| 02500012 | Lenny Kravitz – 5 | $16.95 |
| 02500381 | Lenny Kravitz – Greatest Hits | $14.95 |
| 02503701 | Man of La Mancha | $10.95 |

| | | |
|---|---|---|
| 02500693 | Dave Matthews – Some Devil | $16.95 |
| 02500555 | Dave Matthews Band – Busted Stuff | $16.95 |
| 02500003 | Dave Matthews Band – Before These Crowded Streets | $17.95 |
| 02502199 | Dave Matthews Band – Crash | $17.95 |
| 02500390 | Dave Matthews Band – Everyday | $14.95 |
| 02500493 | Dave Matthews Band – Live in Chicago 12/19/98 at the United Center | $14.95 |
| 02502192 | Dave Matthews Band – Under the Table and Dreaming | $17.95 |
| 02500681 | John Mayer – Heavier Things | $16.95 |
| 02500563 | John Mayer – Room for Squares | $16.95 |
| 02500081 | Natalie Merchant – Ophelia | $14.95 |
| 02500423 | Natalie Merchant – Tigerlily | $14.95 |
| 02502895 | Nine | $17.95 |
| 02500425 | Time and Love: The Art and Soul of Laura Nyro | $19.95 |
| 02502204 | The Best of Metallica | $17.95 |
| 02500407 | O-Town | $14.95 |
| 02500010 | Tom Paxton – The Honor of Your Company | $17.95 |
| 02507962 | Peter, Paul & Mary – Holiday Concert | $17.95 |
| 02500145 | Pokemon 2.B.A. Master | $12.95 |
| 02500026 | The Prince of Egypt | $16.95 |
| 02500660 | Best of Bonnie Raitt | $17.95 |
| 02502189 | The Bonnie Raitt Collection | $22.95 |
| 02502230 | Bonnie Raitt – Fundamental | $17.95 |
| 02502139 | Bonnie Raitt – Longing in Their Hearts | $16.95 |
| 02502088 | Bonnie Raitt – Luck of the Draw | $14.95 |
| 02507958 | Bonnie Raitt – Nick of Time | $14.95 |
| 02502190 | Bonnie Raitt – Road Tested | $24.95 |
| 02502218 | Kenny Rogers – The Gift | $16.95 |
| 02500072 | Saving Private Ryan | $14.95 |
| 02500197 | SHeDAISY – The Whole SHeBANG | $14.95 |
| 02500414 | Shrek | $14.95 |
| 02500536 | Spirit – Stallion of the Cimarron | $16.95 |
| 02500166 | Steely Dan – Anthology | $17.95 |
| 02500622 | Steely Dan – Everything Must Go | $14.95 |
| 02500284 | Steely Dan – Two Against Nature | $14.95 |
| 02500165 | Best of Steely Dan | $14.95 |

| | | |
|---|---|---|
| 02500344 | Billy Strayhorn: An American Master | $17.95 |
| 02502132 | Barbra Streisand – Back to Broadway | $19.95 |
| 02500515 | Barbra Streisand – Christmas Memories | $16.95 |
| 02507969 | Barbra Streisand – A Collection: Greatest Hits and More | $17.95 |
| 02502164 | Barbra Streisand – The Concert | $22.95 |
| 02500550 | Essential Barbra Streisand | $24.95 |
| 02502228 | Barbra Streisand – Higher Ground | $16.95 |
| 02500196 | Barbra Streisand – A Love Like Ours | $16.95 |
| 02500280 | Barbra Streisand – Timeless | $19.95 |
| 02503617 | John Tesh – Avalon | $15.95 |
| 02502178 | The John Tesh Collection | $17.95 |
| 02503623 | John Tesh – A Family Christmas | $15.95 |
| 02505511 | John Tesh – Favorites for Easy Piano | $12.95 |
| 02503630 | John Tesh – Grand Passion | $16.95 |
| 02500124 | John Tesh – One World | $14.95 |
| 02500307 | John Tesh – Pure Movies 2 | $16.95 |
| 02500565 | Thoroughly Modern Millie | $17.95 |
| 02500576 | Toto – 5 of the Best | $7.95 |
| 02502175 | Tower of Power – Silver Anniversary | $17.95 |
| 02502198 | The "Weird Al" Yankovic Anthology | $17.95 |
| 02502217 | Trisha Yearwood – A Collection of Hits | $16.95 |
| 02500334 | Maury Yeston – December Songs | $17.95 |
| 02502225 | The Maury Yeston Songbook | $19.95 |

**See your local music dealer or contact:**

**CHERRY LANE
MUSIC COMPANY**
6 East 32nd Street, New York, NY 10016

*Quality in Printed Music*

EXCLUSIVELY DISTRIBUTED BY

**HAL•LEONARD®**
CORPORATION
7777 W. BLUEMOUND RD. P.O. BOX 13819 MILWAUKEE, WI 53213

Prices, contents and availability subject to change without notice.

0404